FARM
TRACTORS

FARM
TRACTORS

Bill Holder and John D. Farquhar

Crescent Books
New York/Avenel, New Jersey

This 1997 edition published by Crescent Books, distributed by Random House Value Publishing, Inc., 40 Engelhard Avenue Avenel, New Jersey 07001

Random House
New York • Toronto • London • Sydney • Auckland

Produced by
Brompton Books Corporation,
15 Sherwood Place
Greenwich, CT 06830

ISBN 0-517-15932-5

8 7 6 5 4 3 2 1

Printed and bound in China

http://www.randomhouse.com/

Library of Congress Cataloging-in-Publication Data

Holder, William G., 1937-
    Farm tractors/by Bill Holder and John D. Farquhar.
        p. cm.
    Includes index.
    ISBN 0-517-15932-5
    1. Farm tractors – United States – History. I. Farquhar, John D.
II. Title.
TL233.8.F37H65 1997   96-47205
629.225'2 – dc21   CIP

Acknowledgments

The authors would like to thank the following people for their invaluable assistance in the compilation of this book: Dennis Garbig, Manager, AGCO dealership, Greenville, Ohio; Judith Czelusniak, Allison Hopkey, Public Relations, AGCO Corporation; Larry Cruger, North American Equipment Dealership Association; Bill Fogerty, foreign tractor expert; Dennis Alford, Ohio Farm and Power Association; R. D. Farquhar, toy tractor collector and archivist; Jim Vinton, Gene Hemphill, New Holland, Inc.; Ellen Robinson, Case-IH Public Relations; and Al Higley, John Deere Public Relations.

All photographs are by John Farquhar and Bill Holder except for the following:

AGCO: 1, 2, 18(bottom), 37(top), 38, 45, 51(top).
Ken Hawkins: 37(bottom).
Midwest Old Threshers Museum: 44(top).
Andrew Morland: 25(top), 33, 46(top), 47(bottom), 52(top), 53, 54(top).
Collection of C.H. Wendel: 35(upper right inset).

Page 1: A modern White 6085 tractor prepares for the work ahead.

Previous pages: This 5680 AGCO Allis tractor is in the process of doing some heavy mowing.

Right: The Cockshutt 40 was one of the real workhorses during its day. It was produced during the years the company was owned by the Oliver Division of White Motor Corporation.

Contents

Foreword

To any farmer who tills the soil for a living, it's easy to see why the sight of a muddy tractor, old but reliable, is a thing of real beauty.

For the rest of us, the beauty of a tractor might not be so readily apparent. Yet, as we travel on the highways, we are fascinated by the sight of a red Massey-Ferguson tractor, looking like an oversized child's toy chugging away on a vast field.

Perhaps it's because the farm is one of the few places left where we can still find a sense of continuity. Indeed, AGCO was founded in 1990 because we and our customers shared a deep faith in the endurance of the farm equipment business.

As AGCO has grown to become a global force in the agricultural industry, we have remained dedicated to farm equipment. Through our focus on this incredible industry, we now sell more than a dozen trusted brands of farm equipment and we have built the largest network of farm equipment dealers and distributors in the world.

The farm equipment of today and the new technology powering it makes it possible to feed more people than ever before. As the world's population continues to increase, the demands placed on these tractors will become even greater. Agriculture, perhaps the oldest industry in the world, is once again increasing in importance.

In a time when technology moves at a rapid pace and design can become obsolete so quickly, where can true beauty be found? I believe the answer is that beauty can be found in those things that endure. I believe the answer can be found, in some part, on these next pages.

Robert J. Ratliff
Chairman, President, CEO
AGCO Corporation

The tremendous advances made in the mechanization of agriculture over the past century have played a significant role in sustaining the industry's ability to provide an ever-increasing population with food and fiber. No single product has had greater impact on this mechanization than the farm tractor, the machine that has removed much of the backbreaking labors of farming. New Holland is proud of the contributions made by its Ford tractors, and we look forward to making even more contributions with our tractors in the future as a core business of the Fiat Group.

New Holland celebrated its 100th birthday in 1995. The company began a century ago as a small machine shop in New Holland, Pennsylvania, with only a couple of products, a grain mill, and a gasoline engine. Now, a century later, as the largest manufacturer of agricultural tractors in the world, New Holland has its vision fixed on even greater advances, with technology such as robotics and global positioning, as we move into the 21st century.

So enjoy the past and look forward to the future as you turn these pages. As the needs of agriculture continue to be more demanding, the machines being designed today will be ready to meet the challenges.

W. T. Kennedy
Chief Operating Officer
New Holland North America, Inc.

Introduction

The farm tractor is largely a product of the 20th century. The development, advances and refinements of the motorized workhorse have followed the growth of America. Companies have come and gone, both blooming and withering, in their attempt to build the ultimate farm tractor. Without the tractor, America certainly could never have grown as it has.

Farm tractors today compete in an ever-changing world market. Companies are subject to corporate mergers, and as in other industries have also been subject to the current trend toward downsizing. The tractor industry through the years has been particularly fluid. Interestingly, the tractor industry never seemed to adopt the technological advances made by the growing automotive industry. The tractor companies always thought their ways were best, and that was the direction they took.

Today's high-tech farm tractor can trace its roots to the late 19th century. From the invention of steam traction engines and portable gas engines, the tractor began a slow, awkward growth. While the advent of gas-powered tractors gave birth to several new companies like Huber, International Harvester, Hart-Parr, Advance-Rumely, and others, many of the steam tractor builders began to switch to gas. This was the era of single gear machines which were low, often extremely low, on power.

By the 1920s, the tractor market boomed with several hundred factories competing for the farmer's dollar. It is interesting to note that there have been over 900 manufacturers of farm tractors in the United States in the 20th century. With so much competition, many companies failed. Other companies boasted better performance than their machines were capable of in order to attempt to survive. Today, there are only five corporations marketing American-built farm tractors.

Page 7: The grandfathers of today's tractors were the steam-driven machines of the late 19th and early 20th century, which are now only seen at antique tractor shows.

Previous pages: The C.M. Russell Co. of Massilon, Ohio, produced steam traction engines through the mid-1920s.

Left: The A. D. Baker Company of Swanton, Ohio, first produced steam-powered machines, but then turned to gas tractors (like this one) in the 1920s. These early gas tractors produced from 22 to 67 horsepower. The company ended production during World War II.

Opposite: Over 56,000 Advance-Rumely tractors were built between 1904 and 1931. The most popular was the powerful OilPull series, which began production in 1910. This particular model was built in the 1920s and featured a solid flywheel. The company was bought by Allis-Chalmers in 1931.

In 1920, the state of Nebraska passed into law the Nebraska Tractor Test. A company wanting to sell tractors in the state first had to have its product tested. This was perhaps one of the first "Truth in Advertising" laws in the country. Although various forms of tests had been done since 1908, the Nebraska tests were more uniform. Updated over the years, the Nebraska tests have remained the guide for true tractor performance.

The 1920s also saw growth in horsepower, and kerosene-powered machines began to give way to those fueled by gasoline. The ranks of manufacturers began to thin out.

The 1930s saw certain aspects of tractor manufacture become more standardized, such as drawbar height. Tractors also began to look more like today's machines. Pneumatic tires were introduced in 1932 as an option, while steel wheels were still favored by many until the end of World War II. This decade also brought the Depression, which had a great effect on tractor production – 70,000 were built in 1931, but just over 18,000 were manufactured in 1932. The number of companies producing tractors dropped to about 20, with only the strong surviving. Improvements came in power take-offs and driveshafts, and the diesel engine was introduced. Also, the first enclosed cab was introduced by Minneapolis-Moline, but did not immediately gain acceptance by frugal farmers.

The 1930s closed with the introduction of the Ford 9N,

which resulted from an agreement between Harry Ferguson and Henry Ford. The little Ford, with its innovative three-point hitch system developed by Ferguson, and its offspring became possibly the most popular tractors in history.

The 1940s brought several new models from John Deere, Massey-Harris, J.I. Case, and Minneapolis-Moline, but the outbreak of World War II in 1941 brought farm tractor production to a near standstill. Many companies were converted to the war effort. Even the Nebraska tests were terminated, and did not resume until 1946.

When the war was over, there was a worldwide demand for tractors. However, it took over a year to convert back to civilian production. Many new companies jumped into the open market, as demand far exceeded the supply. Even Willys-Overland, builders of the famed Jeep, got into the act with the Universal Jeep: Changes in gearing, transmission, and the addition of a three-point hitch put it into the farm tractor market. Dodge also offered farmers a similar version of its Power Wagon. By 1948, production had surged to over three quarters of a million tractors. This included standard, track-driven and an assortment of walk-behinds and garden tractors.

From 20 companies in 1932, the field grew to over 140 by 1950. Some were short-lived ventures, while others were later absorbed by larger companies. The 1950s were also marked by many new models and the drive was on for better performance, more horsepower, and increased reliability. Designers also began to address such issues as safety and operator comfort. Diesel power became the rule and kerosene tractors were phased out.

Below: The Duplex Machine Company of Battle Creek, Michigan, began producing Co-op tractors in 1936. The high-quality machines, built from stock parts, were sold through several distributors. This Co-op E-4, probably built by Cockshutt, is of a 1940s vintage. The name would vanish shortly thereafter.

Right: This McCormick-Deering tractor is typical of the thousands of similar tractors built from 1923 until 1939. Pneumatic tires were an option on this tractor, as was a power take-off shaft.

Overleaf: Wards Twin-Row tractors were offered via mail order catalog during the early 1940s. A number of different manufacturers produced this model, selling it under the Wards name as well as other names.

Above: Left to right: the Cockshutt 40, the Ford 4630, and the John Deere Model A.

Left: Some models of Co-op tractors were not manufactured by a tractor company. Tractors like this Model C were built under contract between farmers' unions and industrial machine companies.

Opposite: This John Deere Model D heads a line of vintage Deere tractors. This model was built during the 1930s and 1940s. Horsepower was an amazingly low 30.77. Carrying a two-cylinder engine, the Model D proved to be a favorite with farmers.

The 1960s saw four-wheel drive tractors gaining in popularity, and other innovations such as turbo-charging, power steering and brakes, heating and air conditioning were introduced. International Harvester's Model 4300 produced over 300 horsepower in a monumental increase over the first Nebraska-tested machines, which produced only 16 horsepower. There was also a great deal of company consolidation in the 1960s, with White Motors Company buying out such industry giants as Oliver, Cockshutt and Minneapolis-Moline.

The 1970s saw the continued emphasis on horsepower along with comfort and convenience. But the downward spiral of the economy in the early 1980s hit the agricultural community especially hard. A reverse of the situation in the late 1940s took place – the supply now greatly exceeded the demand for new tractors. Many companies merged, with the resulting companies being leaner and meaner. By the 1990s only five companies were still offering the buyer a full line of light-to-heavy duty farm tractors.

To address the high cost of today's new tractors, a number of upgrade programs are available in which a more powerful engine can be put into an older tractor. This service can save the farmer tens of thousands of dollars over the purchase of a new tractor, many of which can reach into the six-figure category.

Even with the high technology of today's tractors, there is a great nostalgic interest in the older machines. Attending antique tractor shows and collecting vintage machines have become popular pastimes. Many antique tractor and thresher shows feature hundreds of examples of the mechanical plowhorse, from the original steam tractors to current production machines. The restoration of old tractors has spurred a cottage industry in parts, manuals, reproduction decals and other items pertaining to the vintage machines.

Scale model and toy tractors are also extremely popular with collectors today. Limited production runs of originals keep collectors on their toes, and originals from the 1950s and earlier bring premium prices. Most of the models are $1/26$ scale, but can be as small as $1/64$ scale.

Tractors have even made their way into the world of

motorsports. The sport of pulling began many decades ago when farmers wanted to see who had the strongest team of horses, and eventually the competition shifted to tractors. The first pulls, in which the tractor pulled a flat sled, were a bit crude. As the sled went down the track, the driver would step on the device at various intervals until there was enough weight to bring the tractor to a stop. But just as tractors have evolved, so has the sport of pulling. Today, the sled is mechanized using a chain-driven weight box which very accurately applies the weight to the tractor.

The most popular professional pulls are conducted by the National Tractor Pulling Association (NTPA) in the United States and the World Pulling Association (WPA) abroad.

While the United States has moved away from its roots as primarily a rural, agricultural nation, the interest in tractors has not waned. The future should be exciting as manufacturers find new ways to improve the tractor. Computers and robotics will certainly play a part in the next century of tractor design.

Above: With considerable modifications, this Massey-Ferguson 2805 is participating in a tractor pull.

Left: The Massey-Ferguson 399's six-cylinder engine provides 90 horsepower directed by a 12-speed transmission. It is available in both two- and four-wheel drive.

Opposite: The 9030 New Holland Ford Versatile tractor, built in Canada, is a four-wheel drive, articulated machine. The tractor uses a Cummins diesel engine. The Versatile Company was purchased by Ford in 1989.

John Deere

John Deere is the only tractor company today that retains its originator's complete name on the hood. Deere's colors, a characteristic green detailed in yellow, still remain the popular brand's trademark and the company has tens of thousands of satisfied customers that swear by the brand.

The John Deere Company began producing steel plows in 1836. Interestingly, the company didn't choose to get into the steam tractor business, but realized during the early 1900s that it was imperative to get into the gas-powered tractor business.

During the 1920s, the company brought out what would prove to be one of the most popular tractors ever – the Model D, which would roll off the production line in continuously improved models until the 1950s.

Another classic Deere machine produced during the same period was the Model A, which was built from 1934 through 1952. The most popular model ever from John Deere, it featured adjustable wheel treads and a one-piece transmission case. The first Model A was rated at only 24 brake horsepower, but that value would be increased several times during its production period.

The Model B, originally rated at only nine drawbar horsepower, was built from 1935 to 1952. A modified version of the B, the Model BO, was built during the 1930s and 1940s, and in the latter part of its production it was equipped with crawler tracks. Later the company would produce the MC model, built from scratch to be a crawler machine.

In 1949, John Deere came out with its first diesel tractor,

Left: The Deere General Purpose Model A was the backbone of the John Deere tractor line from 1934 until 1952. Sporting a two-cylinder 30 horsepower engine, the Model A weighed almost 5,300 pounds.

Opposite top left: The John Deere two-cylinder Model D packed a lot of power into its compact design.

Opposite top right: A close-up of an early John Deere tractor shows the power take-off and drawbar.

Opposite: Vintage John Deeres are very popular among current tractor collectors. Featured in the foreground is a Model L, which today would be considered a compact tractor.

the Model R. The company then began to identify its models with numerals, such as the 20 Series of the mid-1950s, and the 30 Series which replaced it in 1958. The 40, 50, 60, 70, and 80 series replaced previous Deere models throughout the 1950s. Current models are in the 6000 and 7000 series. The company introduced its first four-wheel drive tractor in 1959.

The 40 Series tractors were popular during the 1970s and 1980s. A number of these machines incorporated turbocharged V-6 powerplants producing well in excess of 100 horsepower. The 4955 model of the late 1980s was the first JD tractor to exceed 200 horsepower.

The Model 7800, with its quad rear wheel arrangement, is one of the modern John Deere machines which carries a 466 cubic inch powerplant and produces 170 horsepower, with a transmission that has 20 forward speeds. The Model 6400, one of the top modern four-cylinder John Deere offerings, provides 100 horsepower.

Although the John Deere Company had always been known as a U.S. manufacturer, in the late 1950s the company established production facilities in a number of foreign countries including Argentina, Mexico, Germany, Australia, Africa, Spain, and South Africa. The company also established a relationship with a Japanese company to produce lower-power tractors.

Main photo: The John Deere 50 Series replaced the Model B in 1952. The tractor was available with a gasoline, liquid propane, or tractor all-fuel engine.

Inset, above left: Four decades old, this Model 50 competes in the 1995 Ohio Plowing Championships.

Inset, above: National stock car driver Harris DeVane, accompanied by his son, pushes his John Deere 8400 in a Georgia farm field.

Inset, below: The current John Deere 7800 features a ComfortGard cab, a 145 horsepower turbocharged inline engine, and a 12-speed SyncroPlus transmission.

Ford (New Holland)

The name Ford usually conjures up thoughts of Thunderbirds and Mustangs. But through the decades, Ford has also been a major tractor manufacturer.

Although the Ford name still appears on the famous navy blue machines, the tractor-building arm of the company has undergone a number of changes. In 1986, Ford bought the New Holland Company, and a year later, Ford New Holland purchased the Versatile Tractor Company of Canada. In 1991, Fiat GeoTech became the overall owner. In the mid-1990s, Fiat GeoTech was bought by New Holland, Inc.

Henry Ford's first adventures in tractor building occurred early in the century, and he displayed his first tractor in 1915. The first Ford tractor factory came into being the following year. At the beginning of World War I the British

ordered 5,000 of Ford's machines. The name of the company at the time was Henry Ford and Son, but it would quickly be shortened to Fordson. Some four-fifths of a million Fordsons were produced in the next ten years.

Ford's success in the American car industry was not repeated by its initial tractor venture. Production in the United States ended in 1928, although it was continued under the Ford name overseas. (Ford had opened a production plant in Ireland in 1919, and in 1933, production was transferred to England.) Ford came back on-line in the United States in the 1940s, however, and has maintained a high level of production and technology ever since.

A look at Ford tractors through the years shows that many models introduced new technology and innovations.

Left: With over 100,000 sold per year in the early 1920s, the Fordson Model F was one of America's most successful early tractors.

Below left: This unique-looking 27 horsepower Fordson was converted into a crawler with a Trackpull attachment. The conversion was thought to provide better traction.

Opposite top left: The Ford 9N was introduced in 1939 through an agreement with Harry Ferguson.

Opposite top right: This photo shows a detail of the Ferguson Black three-point hitch. This innovation in tractor design increased versatility in the field.

Opposite: The Ford 9N was followed by models 2N and 8N (shown here). Later models were christened as the 600 Series. The 8N was one of the first post-war tractors to be introduced.

The 1918 version included such improvements as a new high tension magneto, a water pump, and an electric starting system. The 1938 model was Ford's first attempt at a three-wheeled (one in front, two in back) tractor, and also incorporated rubber tires instead of metal wheels.

Also in the late 1930s, a revolutionary development called the three-point system was introduced on Ford's 9N model tractors. The three-point hitch system, designed by Irishman Harry Ferguson, allowed the tractor to be furnished with a variety of implements. The building of these extremely popular tractors would be accomplished jointly

Main photo: The Powermaster series, introduced in the 1950s, featured a four-cylinder 172 cubic inch engine, the first American-built diesel in the Ford tractor line.

Inset, below left: This late 1960s vintage Ford sported a big block six-cylinder engine with over 100 horsepower.

Inset, below right: The Versatile 500 featured a Cummins diesel engine with over 200 horsepower. The four-wheel drive tractors, such as this 1970s model, enabled one operator to handle larger implements, thus cutting down farm costs.

with the Ferguson-Sherman Company, but the association would end in 1946.

For its 50th anniversary in 1953, Ford came out with its modern NAA model. Into the 1960s, Ford had truly become a worldwide producer of many types of tractors. Production was now taking place in India, Brazil, and England, as well as in a number of plants in the United States.

During the 1960s and 1970s, a number of innovative machines were introduced, including the Model 8000, the first tractor carrying the Ford label to mount a 100 horsepower powerplant. The big block 401 cubic inch engine had a similar displacement to the engines of the powerful muscle cars of the era.

In the mid-1970s, several completely new lines, the 600 and 700 series, hit the dealer showrooms. The evolution of the Ford tractor continued into the 1980s with more improvements being made to the powertrains, and increased emphasis on driver comfort, resulting in improved cabs.

After its purchase of Versatile, the company continued production of those machines, the top model of which was the Model 1156 which included a huge 1156 cubic inch turbo-charged Cummins diesel powerplant. The newest line from Ford is the Genesis series of tractors, which offer front-end steering, fuel economy, and driver comfort.

Above: The Power Shift 8830 featured dual rear wheels and was offered in two models. It carried a 401 cubic inch/170 horsepower diesel engine and had 18 forward and nine reverse speeds, and weighed about 15,000 pounds.

Left: The 4630 sports a 201 cubic inch/55 horsepower engine and weighs over $2^{1}/_{2}$ tons.

Opposite: The Ford 8970, in the new Genesis Series, brings high technology to the farm field. The four-wheel drive machines have an innovative and improved steering system. The highest horsepower available in a Genesis model is 210, from a turbocharged intercooled diesel engine.

Caterpillar

The "Cat" brand has long been characterized by its yellow color and its tracked means of locomotion, as opposed to the giant rear tires found on most tractors.

Caterpillar was formed by the merger of two companies – Holt and Best – in 1925. Success came quickly for the new company, with first-year sales of almost $14 million. Three years after its formation, the Russell Grader Company was acquired, bringing graders into the Caterpillar fold.

The first Cat model, the Twenty, appeared in 1927. The Model Thirty had a minimal horsepower of only 30, but with the capability to exert over 7,500 pounds of pulling power. The Model Sixty, developed during the same period, weighed in at ten tons and could pull over 12,300 pounds. In 1931, the company was the first to introduce diesel power in a crawler tractor. The Model Seventy was introduced in the mid-1930s and provided six forward and two reverse

Above: The current Caterpillar Challenger is the only farm tractor using all-track power, which aids in reduced soil compaction.

Left: The Model 75C Challenger carries a 629 cubic inch engine, providing a mammoth 325 horsepower. Its operating weight exceeds 16 tons.

Opposite top: Holt merged with the Best Company in 1925 to form Caterpillar. This small Holt of the 1920s was a forerunner of today's Cat.

Opposite: The Model 65C is the smallest tractor in the Challenger line. Weighing 32,875 pounds, the model is powered by a 638 cubic inch engine producing 285 horsepower.

speeds. The machine grossed out at well over 30,000 pounds and sold for $4,750.

During the late 1940s and early 1950s, the company produced three large tractors sporting adjustable track widths. The models were called the D6, D7, and D8, with the largest, the D8, priced at almost $7,000. These tractors were used by the Combat Engineers during the Korean War. With their low centers of gravity thanks to the heavy tracks, Caterpillar tractors have always been ideally suited for operation on steep hillsides.

One of the newest Cat tractors is the Challenger 65, a true farm tractor. The design of the tractor allows it to provide twice the ground traction of a conventional wheeled tractor, with only one-third of the ground pressure. The 65 boasts 285 horsepower which is acquired at only 2100 rpm. A significant innovation on this modern machine is the "Mobil-trac System" which uses a belt with steel cables serving in four layers. The system provides a ground pressure of only six pounds per square inch because of the large area over which the weight is applied.

AGCO Allis

One of the long-time giants in the U.S. tractor industry was the Allis-Chalmers Company, which dated back to the turn of the century. In 1985, Allis-Chalmers was acquired by a West German company, Klockner-Humboldt-Deutz AG, which renamed its tractor division Deutz-Allis. In 1990, Deutz-Allis was acquired by an American-based holding company, the Allis Gleaner Company (AGCO). The former Allis-Chalmers arm was renamed AGCO Allis.

The Allis-Chalmers Company was formed in 1901 from the merger of four other companies. The company's first tractor was built in 1918. Through the 1930s, the company continued to procure a number of other prestigious companies including the Advance-Rumely Thresher Company, and in 1955, the Gleaner Harvester Corporation.

Allis-Chalmers produced a number of significant tractors through the years. The Model 18-30 was introduced in 1919, and over the next ten years 16,000 were produced.

The Model B is a well-known classic tractor that was built for two decades starting in 1937. Its four-cylinder engine produced just 15.68 brake horsepower, but it was just what was needed by many buyers and 127,186 made the purchase. The price in 1940 was only $518.

The WD-45 model came out after World War II and was available in both gasoline and diesel engine versions. Over 83,000 were produced. With a shipping weight of only 3,900 pounds, the model had a drawbar pull capability of over 4300 pounds.

In the late 1950s, Allis-Chalmers began production of its D Series, which included the D-10, D-12, D-14, D-15,

Left: The Allis-Chalmers Model A was built between 1936 and 1942. It had four forward speeds and sold for $1,495, making it fairly expensive for the time period.

Below: Allis-Chalmers entered the tractor business in 1914 with its Model 10-18, and the smaller Model 6-12 (shown here) appeared five years later. It was produced until 1923.

Main photo: This Ohio farmer was proud to bring his 1963 Allis-Chalmers D-15 to the Ohio Plowing Championships in 1995. The tractor featured a 46 horsepower power take-off capability and weighed about two tons.

Inset, top right: The 1956 Allis-Chalmers WD-45 was the first tractor with factory installed power steering and was powered by a 230 cubic inch diesel engine.

Inset, below right: The AC-185 tractor of the 1970s carried a powerful 301 cubic inch engine capable of 75 HP. It was well known as the Crop Hustler, and many can still be found in the fields in the 1990s.

D-17, D-19, and D-21. The final A-C product was constructed in the mid-1980s.

When A-C was acquired, the parent company retained the Allis portion of the name. The Deutz-Allis tractors were very similar to the A-C machines which had preceded them. One of the most significant of the new tractors, which were built in Germany, was the Model 9130 which sported four rear wheels and was powered by an air-cooled diesel engine.

When AGCO took over, it also chose to retain the Allis name, creating AGCO Allis. In the 1990s, a whole family of AGCO Allis tractors are on the market with horsepower levels from 40 to 215. The 4600 series (40 to 52 horsepower) comes in both two- and four-wheel drive and is the company's smallest tractor line. The family then grows through the 5600, 6600, 7600, 9600, and 9800 series tractors.

Opposite: The little-known Deutz-Allis brand would be discontinued in 1988 after only two years of production. AGCO would then absorb the company and the brand would disappear.

Opposite bottom: A 1995 AGCO Allis 8630 is shown running a seed drill. The 8630 has a six-cylinder air-cooled diesel engine capable of 120 horsepower.

Right: The two modern AGCO Allis tractors shown here, the 5660 and the 5650, are powered by four-cylinder diesel engines with from 63 to 80 horsepower capabilities.

Below right: The powerhouses of the AGCO Allis line are the articulated four-wheel drive tractors. The big diesel engine brings a tremendous capability to the farm field.

AGCOSTAR

In 1995, the tractor industry saw the introduction of a whole new line of tractors and a new name. Not surprisingly, it was the AGCO company which would bring on the new line.

The new Models 8350 and 8425 were specifically designed with the latest in engineering technology to provide for the needs of the large-acreage producer. Both the 8350, rated at 350 horsepower, and the 8425, rated at 425 horsepower, offered a clean design and sloping hood with the muffler and exhaust located on the side of the cab for an unobstructed view.

Under the sleek styling of these new machines is a massive "C" channel high-strength steel front frame with pivoting ball joints providing extra flexibility for a smooth ride and increased wheel traction. The full 35 degrees of steering makes for easier handling.

Two different engines are available for the models – the Detroit Diesel Series 60 engine or a Cummins N14 engine. These are huge powerplants with the Series 60 displacing 744 cubic inches, while the N14 is a monstrous 855 cubic inch engine.

The advanced tractors also sport 18 forward and two reverse speed transmissions that provide seven working gears in the field operation range of three to eight miles per hour. The power is distributed equally between the front and rear tires. The working end of the tractors relies on both a strong, wide swing hitch and large capacity hydraulics. A heavy alloy steel drawbar pivots from the midpoint of the rear frame, swinging on two rollers to eliminate drawbar wear.

Below: The AGCOSTAR 8425, introduced in 1995, is pushed by a big 425 horsepower engine. Two engines are available with the same power, a 744 cubic inch Detroit Diesel and a 855 cubic inch Cummins Diesel.

Right: The AGCOSTAR series of tractors offers improved operator comfort while the working end of the tractor relies on a high-capacity flow and pressure-compensated hydraulic system.

White (AGCO)

White became a force in the tractor industry in the 1960s when it acquired several historic companies. The White Motor Corporation purchased the Oliver Corporation in 1960, retaining the Oliver name and continuing the popular Oliver "55" series through the decade. Oliver had been a leader in the tractor business since 1929, when it was assembled from four companies – Oliver Chilled Plow Works (which dated back to 1868), Hart-Parr, Nichols & Shepard and the American Seeding Machine Company. The characteristic green and yellow machines introduced a number of technical innovations through the years.

In 1962, White purchased the Cockshutt Farm Equipment Company. Cockshutt, one of the pioneers in the business, had roots stretching back to 1839. The final White

Above: Two early giants in the farming industry – Oliver and Hart-Parr – merged in the 1930s, forming the new name shown here. The Row Crop name indicated a tricycle design, which allowed the tractor to go between rows.

Left: The Oliver 90 was originally built in the l930s and developed 49 horsepower with three forward speeds. The tractor weighed just over 3,000 pounds.

Opposite top: The Oliver Row Crop 66 (foreground) and 77 were longtime models in the company lineup from the late 1940s into the l960s. Early versions of these tractors only weighed about 3,200 pounds.

Opposite: The Oliver Super 99 GM carrried a General Motors three-cylinder, two-cycle supercharged, 230 cubic inch diesel engine. The model also was equipped with disc brakes, with a three-point hitch and cab as options.

acquisition was another tractor-building legend – Minne-apolis-Moline, which came on board in 1963. White retained the Oliver, Cockshutt and Minneapolis-Moline names until 1969.

Another business deal took place in 1987 when White and the New Idea Farm Equipment Company merged. It was finally White's turn to be acquired when the AGCO Corporation of Waycross, Georgia, purchased the company in 1991. The White name and colors, however, have been retained.

A number of popular models have evolved from White through recent years, including the Plainsman which fea-

Main photo: This early 1950s Cockshutt Model 40 is shown pulling a two-bottom plow. This Canadian-made tractor had a Buda six-cylinder engine of 230 cubic inches with six forward speeds.

Inset, opposite left: The Cockshutt Model 20, introduced in 1952, used a Continental four-cylinder L-head 140 cubic inch engine. It had four forward speeds and weighed just over 2,800 pounds.

Inset, opposite right: Built in the late 1950s, the Cockshutt Golden Arrow carried a four-cylinder Perkins engine. Note the fancy two-tone paint scheme on this attractive field machine.

Left: The Moline Universal was built from 1915 to 1923. It featured electric starting and lights. The powerplant provided 27 horsepower.

Below: A vintage Minneapolis-Moline Model U is hooking up for an antique tractor pull in 1995. The M-M machines were characterized by their bright yellow paint schemes.

Opposite top: Powered by a 359 cubic inch/124HP Cummins turbocharged diesel engine, the 6125 represents the smallest model in the White Powershift tractor line. It weighs in at just over 15,000 pounds.

Opposite bottom: The White 6215 is the company's flagship in its Powershift series. With a huge 504 cubic inch engine, a direct-injected diesel, it is capable of putting 215 horsepower to the tilling duties.

tured an eight-wheel arrangement and carried a 504 cubic inch gas engine capable of producing 169 horsepower. The Plainsman began production in the early 1970s.

A number of White tractors were marketed under the Field Boss name. The 2-60 model was produced during the late 1970s, but production took place in Italy by Fiat. Later versions of the Field Boss were the 2-70 with a 70 horsepower capability, while the 4-150 carried a 150HP Caterpillar diesel engine under the gray and off-white hood.

New White tractors include the 6125-PFA, 6145-PFA, 6175-2WD, 6195-PFA and 6215-PFA models. These models demonstrate horsepower from 125 up to 215, with the largest model, the 6215, weighing over 17,000 pounds.

Massey-Ferguson (AGCO)

Two tractor companies, Massey-Harris and Ferguson, came together in 1953 to form what would become the Massey-Ferguson Company in 1958. The Canadian-based company produces tractors in many foreign countries, with most of its products going to developing nations.

Like so many other of the former agricultural giants, Massey-Ferguson became a part of the giant AGCO organization, in 1994. The Massey-Ferguson name continues to be used on the line of tractors.

The Massey-Harris Company was established in 1891 in Toronto, Canada. The roots of that organization actually stretched back to 1847, when Daniel Massey started to manufacture farm implements. A. Harris, Son & Company was a strong competitor of Massey's during the latter portion of the 19th century, before the two companies merged.

Many effective tractor models were produced under the Massey-Harris nametag, with the Model 25 being a farm favorite during the early 1930s. The model, which had a maximum of 41 horsepower, remained basically unchanged until after World War II.

Opposite: The Massey-Harris 4WD General Purpose, introduced in 1931, was a four-wheel drive row-crop tractor.

Opposite bottom: This 1935 Massey-Harris 101 illustrates the technology of the period which included a six-cylinder Chrysler engine producing about 24 horsepower. Both steel and rubber tires were available.

Right: During the 1930s, Massey-Harris introduced the classy Twin-Power Challenger. Weighing a hefty 5,900 pounds on rubber tires, the tractor was powered by a M-H four-cylinder I-head engine with about 36 horsepower.

Below: The popular Massey-Harris Model 44 was introduced in 1947. Carrying the same I-head engine as the Challenger, the 44 had five forward speeds and weighed 2^1/$_2$ tons.

The Massey-Harris Model 30 was introduced in 1947 and saw a production run of over 32,000 in the following six years. Featuring a five-speed transmission, the Model 30 was rated as a "two-plow" tractor.

The Ferguson part of the M-F name came from the efforts of Harry Ferguson, who had worked with Henry Ford, and produced a significant number of tractors from the 1930s through the 1950s.

The first tractor built after the Massey-Harris and Ferguson merger was the MF-35, introduced in 1960. It would be followed by a whole new family of tractors including the MF-50, MF-65, and MF-85.

In 1976, the company introduced its advanced 1505 and 1805 models, both of which were powered by a 174 horse-power Caterpillar V-8 diesel engine.

The 3000 Series of the mid-1980s brought electronics to bear with the replacement of the systems that had activated

Opposite top: Weighing in at 5,190 pounds, this 1950s-vintage Massey-Harris 33 developed an impressive 258 pound-feet of torque from its 201 cubic inch powerplant.

Opposite: The Massey-Harris Pony weighed less than a ton and had only ten horsepower. Today, it would be considered a small riding mower.

Above: Built by Harry Ferguson, Inc., this Ferguson TO-30 of the early 1950s very much resembles the early Ford tractors.

Right: Moving away from the normal inline engine style, the Massey-Ferguson 1150 featured a Perkins 510 cubic inch V-8 diesel engine. The engine provided 135 horsepower. Note the dual rear wheels on this 1970s-vintage tractor.

the tractor's hydraulic system. Horsepower was on its way up as demonstrated by the 190HP six-cylinder turbo-charged engine on this machine.

Another significant Massey-Ferguson product was the Model 398 which uses a 236 cubic inch turbo-diesel power-plant and has the capability to engage its four-wheel drive capability on the move.

Possibly the most advanced Massey-Ferguson tractor is the Model 1250. The tractor has an articulated design, which means that the rear wheels are pivoted off the front of the tractor, allowing it to make extremely sharp turns. The model looks more like a semi truck than a tractor. With a sur-prisingly low power capability of only 96 horsepower, the 1250 has 12 forward speeds and four reverse.

Opposite: Developing 33 horsepower from its 138 cubic inch diesel engine, the Massey-Ferguson TO-35 was produced in the late 1950s and early 1960s.

Opposite bottom: Perkins and Waukesha engines were used on various versions of the Massey-Ferguson 1100. The Perkins was a 354 cubic inch diesel, while the Waukesha was a 320 cubic inch gasoline engine.

Right and below: Massey-Ferguson, now a division of AGCO, currently offers the 6100 and 8100 lines. Seen at right is the 6180, and below, the 8120. The tractors feature Perkins engines, closed cabs, and unique gauge displays.

Case-IH

Two of the great names in tractor building – the J.I. Case Threshing Company and the International Harvester Company (IH) – came together in 1984 to form Case-IH, which has become one of the giants in the industry.

The J. I. Case Threshing Company was formed in 1863 to build steam tractors. IH was created in 1902 as the result of a merger of the McCormick and Deering companies.

Both IH and Case were powerful forces in the industry, responsible for a number of technical innovations. The first International Harvester tractors appeared in 1906 when the Type A gasoline tractor was offered with 12, 15, and 20 horsepower engines. The Type B model which followed incorporated a gear drive, and was produced until 1916. During the 1910s, IH produced the gigantic Mogul tractor which sported a 45 horsepower engine, huge for the time. A real innovator, IH produced some interesting experimental

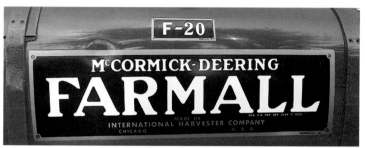

Opposite top: International Harvester's Titan was powered by a 22 horsepower engine. It was produced from 1919 to the early 1920s.

Opposite center: The McCormick and Deering names appeared on International Harvester's popular line of Farmall tractors. The Deering name was later dropped.

Opposite: This Farmall tractor of the late 1930s shows the early rubber-covered steel wheels, a vintage forerunner of the cab, and the primitive steering system of these machines.

Above: International Harvester came out with the big, all-purpose McCormick-Deering WK-40 in 1934.

Right: This photo shows a 1949 Farmall Model M, which produced 34-39 horsepower in several models, and was also available in a "High Crop" version.

Left: The 1949 McCormick Standard W-6 featured four forward speeds and a four-cylinder IH engine with 25 horsepower.

Below: Using kerosene fuel, Case Model C's were built from the late 1920s into the 1930s. The two Cases shown here are early 1930s models.

Opposite top: A 1940s Case Model DC displays an interesting cap.

Opposite bottom: The Case Model DO, the Orchard Model, was so named because the unique fenders and driver's cowl protected valuable fruit trees from damage by the tractor.

models, one of which was a six-wheel drive all-terrain vehicle introduced in the mid-1920s.

Farmall was a popular model name used by International beginning in the 1920s. Probably the best-known model was the Farmall M of the 1950s. Many thousands of those machines were produced, and many are still in the fields in the 1990s. During the 1970s, the 966 Farmall model fea-

tured 16 forward gears and 100 horsepower from a 414 cubic inch powerplant.

Case's first tractor appeared in 1892. The company was one of the leaders in the industry in the early 20th century, and by 1923 had produced 100,000 tractors. The famous Model L, which featured unit frame construction, started production in 1929. The significant Case models produced in more recent times included the 1370 Agri-King which carried a six-cylinder 504 cubic inch turbo-charged diesel. The 1970s-vintage Case 2470 had a power shift transmission and four-wheel steering.

Several exceptional tractors have evolved since the assets of both companies were combined. The magnificent Case-IH 9280 features a design which looks more like that of a semi truck than of a tractor, and features a transmission with 12 forward and three reverse speeds. The advanced tractor can sport as many as six wheels (front or rear) mounted in tandem. Horsepower has come a long way with the intercooled 855ci engine producing 375 horsepower.

A popular late-model Case-IH tractor is the Model 1494, which carries a 3594cc diesel engine. The versatile machine has four types of speeds – creep, field, on-road and reverse.

Main photo: This Case 2390 of 1970s-1980s vintage is busy in an Ohio soybean field in the summer of 1995. It carried a 504 cubic inch diesel powerplant with 160 horsepower.

Below: This I995 Case International Model 7220 Magnum shows 150 horsepower, front drive traction, 10,040-pound hitch lift capability, and a completely computerized engine monitoring system.

Below: The Case International 5250 Maxxum, seen in the front of a line of new Case International tractors, is a mid-size tractor with 112 horsepower from a 359 cubic inch turbocharged diesel engine with direct injection, and a 35 gallon fuel tank.

Foreign Tractors

The first tractors to be imported in the United States were Fordsons, built by Henry Ford, founder of the Ford Motor Company and inventor of the assembly line. The Fordsons were first built in Ireland and shipped to the U.S. starting in 1929. Production was later moved to Birmingham, England. The Fordson name was dropped in the 1960s, but Ford continues to import tractors from England.

The first foreign tractor tested in Nebraska was the British-built Fordson in 1937 and 1938, but a decade would pass before any other imports were offered up for testing. Since 1948, nearly every country in the world that builds tractors has exported tractors to the United States with varying degrees of success.

Past imports from England have included: Ferguson, Nullfield, David Brown, Land Rover, and McCormick International. From Canada, Cockshutt, Versatile, and Massey-Harris have come to the United States. German imports have included Unimog, Porsche, Kramer, and Deutz. Italian tractors have been offered by Fiat, Landini, SAME, Hesston (Fiat), and two companies known specifically for high-performance cars, Ferrari and Lamborghini.

Japanese tractors have been imported from Kubota, Satoh (Mitsubishi), and Yanmar. Japanese-built tractors have also carried American nametags such as John Deere, White, Massey-Ferguson, Allis-Chalmers, Case-IH and Ford.

The Mahindra line, built in India, was once marketed by IH and contained interchangeable parts, while the TAFE was once marketed in the United States under an American name. Two new names from India are Dragon and Zebra, now being imported in the United States, which range in horsepower from 25 to 80.

Of the imports, Kubota has been a strong contender for a number of years, offering a full line of compact two- and four-wheel drive tractors for light-to-medium duty, including a new Grand L series of tractors, featuring an enclosed cab. The Kubotas are known for performance and state-of-the-art design.

Belarus Machinery Inc. has been exporting tractors from

Opposite: The Kubota IC Shuttle M9580 has a 284 cubic inch four-cylinder engine making I00 horsepower. The model features 24 forward and 24 reverse speeds.

Right: The Kubota L4200 is powered by a four-cylinder, 134 cubic inch 37 horsepower engine. This example is pictured equipped with a post-hole digger.

the former Soviet State of Belarus (now a member of the Community of Independent States (CIS)) for 17 years. Belarus offers six series of tractors in 28 configurations, ranging in horsepower from 31 to 180. They keep the machines basic and simple, and stress reliability and economy. The top of the Belarus line is the 1770 180 horsepower articulated tractor for full-size operations.

The Romanian Long tractors come in six models, in both two- and four-wheel drive and range in power from 95 to 229 horsepower.

The Korean Kioti tractors range in horsepower from 19 to 30 and feature three-cylinder water-cooled diesel engines.

The Chinese tractors are marketed under several different names, with Rhino, Shennui and Hardy being the most recognized. This line of tractors is very basic and fits into the compact size group. The Hartford Tractor Company is currently importing a number of these tractors, upgrading them, and then reselling them.

The Czech-built Zetor tractors range from 40 to 160 horsepower and have been exported to America since 1983.

JCB Landpower of England exports a variety of tractors. The line is showcased by the Fastrac l85, which carries a Cummins 185 horsepower six-cylinder engine, along with 36 forward and 12 reverse speeds. It is capable of moving at 40 miles per hour while pulling a 14-ton trailer.

The American manufacturers themselves have long been importing foreign-built tractors. In addition to the aforementioned Japanese machines, John Deere has imported German tractors, while Allis-Chalmers (before being bought by AGCO) imported tractors from both Romania and Italy. AGCO imports Italian tractors from Landini and SAME.

Opposite: The former Soviet Republic contributes the functional Belarus tractor line. This is the 925, which carries a 100 horsepower engine. These tractors have been imported for a number of years.

Above right: The four-wheel drive Rhino series of Chinese tractors offers an affordable option for farmers on a tight budget.

Right: India exports TAFE compact tractors. The 45DI is shown here.

Massey-Ferguson has brought in both French and Italian tractors, and Case-IH has imported tractors from England, Sweden, and Italy. Massey-Ferguson also builds a number of models in Canada which are imported in the United States.

Other tractor brands which have been imported in the United States include Leyland (from Scotland), Volvo (from Sweden), Someca (from France), and Ursus (from Poland).

In an interesting development, the Chinese are currently marketing a tractor in Australia that is approximately 50 percent John Deere parts. The tractors are built in China to Deere specifications for the Australian market.

Imported tractors have long influenced American tractor design and sales, and will certainly affect the industry in the years to come.

Opposite top: Romania exports its Long tractors to the United States. The half-dozen available models cover a wide range in power and size.

Opposite: Without fanfare, many foreign tractors have been imported to the United States through the years. David Brown tractors were imported for a number of years from England.

Above: The JCB brand is imported from England and features extremely versatile machines.

Right: The Landini tractor line is imported from Italy and marketed by AGCO, and offers compact to full-size tractors.

Index

Page numbers in *italics* indicate photographs.